Easy words to read

Shark in the Park

Phil Roxbee Cox

Illustrated by Stephen Cartwright

Edited by Jenny Tyler

Language consultant:
Marlynne Grant
BSc, CertEd, MEdPsych, PhD, AFBPs, CPsychol

There is a yellow duck to find on every page.

First published in 2002 by Usborne Publishing Ltd. Usborne House, 83-85 Saffron Hill, London EC1N 8RT, England. www.usborne.com
Copyright ©2002 Usborne Publishing Ltd.

The name Usborne and the devices ♀ ⊕ are Trade Marks of Usborne Publishing Ltd. All rights reserved. No part of this publication may be reproduced, stored in a retrieval system, or transmitted in any form or by any means electronic, mechanical, photocopying, recording or otherwise, without prior permission of the publisher. UE. Printed in Hong Kong, China. First published in America in 2002

Pup is in the park.

"There's a shark
in the park!"
Pup barks.

7

Pup
wakes
Fat Cat.

She meows,
"Why did
you bark?"

"There's a shark
in the park!"
Pup barks.

"It has a sharp, pointy fin."

Big Pig is lighting a fire.
What a bright spark!

"It has a
sharp, pointy
nose."

Hen is with her pad and pens.
She makes bright squiggles
and marks.

"There's a shark
in the park!"
Pup barks.

"It has sharp,
pointy...

Sam Sheep is asleep,
where it's dark.

"There's a shark
in the park!"
Pup barks.

"A shark?"
meows
Fat Cat.

"A shark?"
grunts
Big Pig.

12

"A shark?" clucks Hen.

"ZZZZZZ," snores Sam Sheep (still fast asleep).

13

"Yes, a shark. There is a SHARK in the PARK!" Pup barks.

"Make your way to the lake!"

14

Up pops Jake Snake.

There's no shark in the park!

It's Jake Snake and his rubber ring!